ON THE MAP

ITALY

Titles in This Series:

France

Italy

Spain

U.S.A.

Series editor: Daphne Butler
American editor: Marian L. Edwards
Design: M&M Partnership
Photographs: ZEFA except
Chris Fairclough 17, 18, 22bl; Robert Harding 27;
Sporting Pictures 22tl
Map artwork: Raymond Turvey
Cover photo: *Venice*

Library of Congress Cataloging-in-Publication Data

Butler, Daphne, 1945–
   Italy / written by Daphne Butler.
      p.   cm. — (On the map)
   Summary: An illustrated introduction to the geography, history,
industries, people, customs, and famous landmarks of Italy.
   ISBN 0–8114–3677–2
   1. Italy — Juvenile literature. [1. Italy.] I. Title.
II. Series.
DG417.B88 1993   92–16649
945—dc20   CIP
                                                   AC

Typeset by Multifacit Graphics, Keyport, NJ
Printed and bound in the United States
1 2 3 4 5 6 7 8 9 0 VH 98 97 96 95 94 93

ITALY

Daphne Butler

RSVP

RAINTREE STECK-VAUGHN
P U B L I S H E R S
The Steck-Vaughn Company

Austin, Texas

Contents

Mountains and Coasts

Italy is in the southern part of Europe. It is a long, thin country that juts out into the Mediterranean Sea. On a map, Italy looks like a tall, high-heeled boot. In addition, Italy has two big islands—Sicily and Sardinia. There are also 70 much smaller islands.

Hills and chains of mountains cover a large part of Italy. In the north, the Alps and the Dolomites separate Italy from the rest of Europe. Another chain of mountains, the Apennines, form a rocky backbone down the entire length of the country.

Italy's coastline is often rough and rocky. In some places steep mountains run right up to the sea. Villages with houses clinging to the rocky cliffs are a common sight. Where there are sandy beaches, the coast is calm and still.

In summer, Italy is hot and sunny. Winters are mostly mild, although there are some cold days. Up in the mountains, in the north, there is snow. Rainfall is heavy in the winter and fall, but very scarce in spring and summer. The lower levels of the Dolomites are covered with forests and meadows, but the peaks are bare and snow-covered most of the year.

The Dolomites near Corvara in winter.
The Dolomites are in the north of Italy.

The volcano is Mount Etna in Sicily.
Sicily is a large island to the south.

The beach at Gatteo a Mare
on the east coast.

The rocky cliffs near La Spezia
in the northwest.

Stresa, a town on Lake Maggiore in the Alps.

Many streams and rivers flow off the mountains to join the River Po.
This is one stream of the Po at Bobbio in Emilia-Romagna.

Lakes and Rivers

A great deal of rain and snow falls on the Alps in winter. The snow melts in the spring and the water collects in mountain lakes. Some of the largest and most beautiful lakes in all of Europe lie partly or entirely in Italy.

The Po is the largest and longest river in Italy. It covers over 400 miles from its beginning in the mountains to its mouth. South of the Alps, the Po River flows across a flat plain, meeting the sea in the east. This broad, fertile plain is known as the Po Valley. It has very good soil and plenty of water. The Po Valley is Italy's only major area of level land. For this reason, it is Italy's main farming region.

Going south from the Po Valley the land becomes drier. The soil is less fertile and the weather is hotter.

In winter many of the rivers entering the plains from the mountains become swollen by rains and the melting snow. This causes flooding and a lot of damage to the farms at the bottom of the mountains. In recent times a system of dikes was built to help control the flooding.

Rome and the Romans

Rome is about half-way down the west coast of Italy. Most of the city is sprawled along the banks of the Tiber River. Rome is the capital and largest city in Italy. It is the home of the government and a major business center.

More than 2,000 years ago, Rome was the center of a huge empire. The Roman Empire covered Western Europe, North Africa, and most of the Middle East. Ancient Rome was a very powerful city, with over a million people.

Today the city combines the old with the new. Ruins of ancient Roman buildings are nestled between more recent buildings. Narrow, twisting streets from an earlier time, open on to broad avenues and piazzas. A piazza is a large plaza or open square.

The Roman Empire helped the spread of Christianity across Europe. Today there is a separate state within Rome called the Vatican. The Vatican takes up almost 110 acres and is in the center of the city. It is the headquarters of the Roman Catholic Church and the home of the Pope. Many Italians are Roman Catholic.

The view over Rome from the Vatican. The Vatican is a separate city-state and the center of the Roman Catholic Church.

The port of Genoa in the northwest—Italy's largest and most important port.

The Doges' Palace in Venice in the northeast of Italy.

The Vecchio Palace and the Uffizi Gallery in Florence.

Other Italian Cities

The north of Italy is the most prosperous part of the country. In the north, Milan, Turin, and Genoa are all big industrial cities. They export goods to the rest of the world.

Milan is the second largest city in Italy. It has many interesting buildings and monuments. It is known around the world as the fashion capital of Italy.

Turin is in the western part of the Po Valley, at the foot of the Alps. It is one of Italy's leading industrial cities. Its factories turn out cars, trucks, and chemicals.

Genoa is on the Mediterranean coast. It is a rugged, hilly port city. Ships from many countries sail in and out of this thriving city.

There are other cities in the north like Venice, Florence, and Pisa. These cities were very important in the past. The people who lived there had new ideas, were very rich, and built beautiful churches and palaces. Florence was the home of many artists during a period of great achievement.

Italian Style

Italy has a rich tradition of art that started a long time ago. Italians have painted some of the world's finest paintings. This tradition is preserved today in the art schools in most Italian cities.

Italian music is enjoyed by people all over the world. The first opera was written in the 17th century. It was quickly accepted by the public. Soon it spread throughout Europe. Today, most of the world's major cities have an opera season.

Italians have built many magnificent buildings. Great domed churches, museums, and palaces are visited by millions of tourists each year. Many of the structures took hundreds of workers many years to build.

Today, Italian design is valued in many industries, especially textiles and cars. People of Italy have made great contributions to both film and the theater. Italian-made clothes and shoes are of high quality and are sold throughout the world. Italian clothes and shoes have become one of Italy's main exports.

We call these traditions Italian-style. Style is a way of doing things that can be easily recognized. Italian style is valued and copied by people around the world.

The way Italians look and behave is at the root of what we call Italian style.

The Piazza Navona in Rome—a mix of history, music, art, and fashion.

The Via Tornabuoni in Florence— the place to go for fashion.

The Family

The family is the most important thing in Italian life. Family members are very close to one another. Most unmarried adult children live at home. A typical household might include parents, children, and grandparents. Children are looked after with great care and affection. They are included in most family activities. Grandparents help care for young children while parents go to work.

Relatives visit each other regularly. They help each other in their business affairs. On Sundays several families will get together for midday dinner. These often last for three hours. After this families may take a stroll through the city.

Most families live in or near the city. They live in apartment buildings or in houses on the outskirts of the city. Many had left the countryside and mountain villages to work in the cities. Someday they hope to return to their villages.

In the south of Italy there is not much industry. Most family farms are small and do not have modern equipment. The land is dry and hard to farm. Life is not easy for these farmers. The strength of the family helps them to manage a very difficult life.

Italian families often live in apartments built in and around towns and cities.

Homes are comfortable with plenty of space for visiting relatives.

A classroom in an Italian elementary school.

Going to School

Schools in Italy are free and run by the government. Children must attend school when they are six years old and stay until they are fourteen. Kindergarten is available, and children as young as three can attend.

Most Italian children attend public schools, although some go to private ones run by the Catholic Church. Children stay in primary school for five years. Then they go to a junior secondary school for three years.

At age fourteen children can leave school, but many go on to senior secondary schools to further their education. Senior secondary schools offer four- or five-year programs. Students can pick from technical, vocational, or many other kinds of training.

Italy has some of the oldest universities in the world. They began long ago in the 13th century. At that time Italian cities were very important places for new ideas.

Any senior secondary school graduate may attend a university. Most universities are public, although the Catholic Church runs a few private ones. Students pay a small fee to attend these schools of higher learning.

Food and Shopping

Italians are known for good cooking. Each region has its own special methods and recipes. The people take great pride in the preparation of food.

Breakfast is a very simple meal. It is mostly coffee or hot chocolate and bread or rolls. Lunch is usually the main meal of the day at midday.

A meal often begins with pasta followed by meat or fish, vegetables, and salad. The meal is finished with dessert or fruit and cheese. Adults drink wine with main meals. Children drink water or fruit juice.

In Italy outdoor restaurants are a common sight. Families and friends gather at restaurants to enjoy a good meal. Coffee bars are also popular. People stand and sip small cups of Italian coffee.

Italy grows plenty of fruits and vegetables. Neighborhood markets and outdoor stands are loaded with apples, peaches, and citrus fruits. Shoppers can also buy fresh vegetables such as tomatoes and beans.

Italy is famous for its meat stores. They sell fresh and smoked meats. There are many kinds of ham, sausage, and bacon. These stores also sell cheeses and olives.

Lunch on the ski slopes in the sunshine.

A food store in Genoa.

Italy played Argentina in the 1990 World Cup Soccer Games held in Italy.

A carnival is held in Venice in late February each year.

Families enjoy doing sports together.

A festival in Siena—time to share a new idea.

Leisure Time

Italians enjoy getting together with their relatives and friends. Social occasions are a very important part of their lives.

Most Italian homes have television sets. Watching television is probably the most important pastime. There are about ten national channels and about 500 local television stations.

Another favorite pastime is going to the piazza. Most city neighborhoods have a piazza, often with a church nearby. It is a good place to stroll around or to sit and watch the people. Someone is always playing a guitar or an accordian. Groups of boys play soccer, while younger children jump rope. No place is more popular for meeting friends. For many Italians, life would not be the same without the piazza.

Italians love sports. Soccer is a passionate national interest. So are car racing and cycling. Italians also enjoy a variety of other sports such as tennis, basketball, fishing, and skiing.

August is when most people take their vacations. Families often take their vacations together. Most families go to the east coast or to the mountains.

Farming and Fishing

About one third of the land in Italy is used as farmland. Italy grows almost enough fruits, vegetables, and grains to feed its own people. Farmers raise cattle, sheep, pigs, and chickens. But this is not enough for all the people in Italy. Meat has to be imported from other countries.

The main farming region is in the north in the Po Valley. Here good soil and plenty of water produce grains, fruit, and vegetables. There are also vineyards on the slopes of the Alps and Dolomites. Italy is among the world's leading producers of wine.

Farther south, the land is usually much poorer and drier. Yet there are pockets of fertile soil. Here farmers grow oranges, lemons, grapes, and olives. Olives grow especially well in this kind of soil. They are used for their fruit as well as their oil.

Italy's coasts produce a wealth of seafood. Sicily has the largest fishing industry in Italy. Sardine and tuna fishing are important industries. The Mediterranean waters also provide the people with shrimp and anchovies.

Italy has the world's biggest olive crop.

Fishing boats in Catania harbor in Sicily.

Vineyards by Lake Garda in the Alps.

Rice fields in the Po Valley in the north.

Industry

Most Italian industries are in the northwest, near Genoa, Turin, and Milan. Factories in these cities process iron, steel, chemicals, textiles, automobiles, and trucks.

There are also many food processing factories. Fruits and vegetables are bottled, canned, and preserved. Sugar beets are refined, and over a hundred varieties of pasta are made.

Milan, Rome, and Florence are centers for the fashion industry. Fine crystal and glassware are also produced in these cities. In addition, the production of films and motion pictures is big business. Countless motion pictures are made in and around Italy's cities.

Many of the things Italy produces are used by its people. However, it sells large quantities of Italian food, clothes, chemicals, and cars to other countries. Italian clothes are one of the country's biggest exports.

Tourism is still one of Italy's greatest industries. Its cities and towns receive millions of visitors each year. Italy's islands and beaches are favorite places for vacationers.

The Fiat automobile plant in Turin. Car engines are assembled by robots.

Leather coats ready for sale in Milan.

Famous Landmarks

The Swiss guard are mercenary troops paid by the Vatican to guard the gates.

The leaning bell tower at Pisa was built in the 12th century. It is 180 feet high and leans 16 feet from the vertical.

Florence seen from the Michelangelo park. Michelangelo was an artist and sculptor who lived in the 16th century.

Venice is built on a lagoon and is in danger of sinking into the sea. St. Mark's Piazza at high tide.

The ruins of the forum in Rome. Roman cities always had a meeting place where the business of the city was carried out.

Facts and Figures

Italy-the Land and People

Population	57,800,000
Area	116,320 square miles
Distance northwest to southeast	311 miles
Capital city	Rome
Population	2,850,000
Language	Italian
Religion	Roman Catholic

Main Public Holidays

New Year's Day	January 1
Easter Monday	date varies
Liberation Day	April 25
May Day	May 1
Tricolor Day	May 12
Assumption	August 15
All Saints' Day	November 1
National Unity Day	November 5
Immaculate Conception	December 8
Christmas Day	December 25
St. Stephen's Day	December 26

Hours and Money

School hours	9 A.M. to 12:30 P.M. 3:30 P.M. to 6 P.M. Monday to Friday
Shopping and business hours	9 A.M. to 12:30 P.M. 3:30 P.M. to 8:00 P.M. shops closed Sunday and often Monday
Money	Lira 1,176 lira are about $1.00

Landmarks

Highest mountain	Monte Rosa in the Alps 15,200 ft.
Longest river	River Po
Active volcanoes	Etna Stromboli

Some Useful Italian Words

hello	ciao	yes	si
good-bye	ciao	no	no
please	per favore	mister	signor
thank you	grazie	madam	signora

Average Temperatures in Fahrenheit

	January	June
Milan (northwest)	34°F	72°F
Venice (northeast)	37°F	69°F
Palermo (south)	50°F	75°F

Further Reading

Non-Fiction

Anno, Mitsumasa. *Anno's Italy*. Philomel, Putnam Publishing Group, 1984

Bonomi, Kathryn. *Italy*. Chelsea House, 1991

Fairclough, Chris. *Take a Trip to Italy*. Watts, 1981

Mariella, Cinzia. *Passport to Italy*. Watts, 1986

Fiction

Brown, Regina. *Little Brother*. Astor, 1962

Henry, Marguerite. *Gaudenzia Pride of the Palio*. Macmillan Children's Group, 1989

Index

©1991 Simon & Schuster Young Books